The Usborne
Little Book of Garden
Wildlife

First published in 2006 by Usborne Publishing Ltd.,
Usborne House, 83-85 Saffron Hill, London EC1N 8RT, England.
www.usborne.com

Printed in Dubai

The Usborne
Little Book of Garden
Wildlife

Laura Howell

Designed by Michael Hill,
Laura Hammonds and Kate Rimmer
Digital illustration by Keith Furnival

Consultants: Jenny Steel and
Dr Margaret Rostron

Edited by Kirsteen Rogers

Internet links

There are lots of fun websites where you can find out more about garden wildlife. We have created links to some of the best sites on the Usborne Quicklinks Website. To visit the sites, go to www.usborne-quicklinks.com and type the keywords "little garden wildlife". Here are some of the things you can do on the Internet:

✻ Plan your own virtual wildlife garden
✻ Find out how to make bird cakes and feeders
✻ Pick up lots of tips for attracting animals to your garden

Wildlife pictures to download

Pictures marked with a ✱ in this book can be downloaded from the Usborne Quicklinks Website. These pictures are for personal use only and must not be used for commercial purposes.

Internet safety

The websites recommended in Usborne Quicklinks are regularly reviewed. However, the content of a website may change at any time and Usborne Publishing is not responsible for the content of websites other than its own. We recommend that children are supervised while on the Internet.

Respecting nature

When it comes to nature, it's better to look rather than touch. A bird's nest that appears to be empty might be used again by its maker in a different season, and flowers should always be left where they're growing for everyone to enjoy. You should never try to pet wild animals, or touch their droppings.

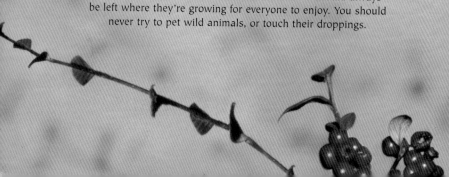

Contents

Garden wildlife

To many people, a garden is just a place to relax and
have fun. But to animals, it's a breeding ground,
food store and hideaway rolled into one.

Living together

All animals rely on
plants, or other animals,
for food. The many
creatures that feed
together in a garden
show how things
in nature are linked.

Butterflies and bees
feed from flowers.

Ladybirds eat
tiny bugs that
live on plants.

Bringing up babies

Most animals need a place to find
a mate and have babies. A garden's
varied landscape is ideal for this,
giving them protection and often
a source of food for their family, too.

Gardens supply birds
with a place to nest, and
worms to feed their chicks.

Ideal homes

A place that has all the things an animal needs to survive is called a habitat. A garden is full of different habitats, each one with just the right conditions for something to live there.

Some insects build their nests in holes in walls.

Wall mason wasp

Look in soil and under rocks for scuttling animals such as woodlice.

Centipede

Woodlouse

Rotting compost is home to worms, beetles and centipedes.

Garden snail

Flowerbeds offer shelter to snails, slugs and caterpillars.

A helping hand

Although it's enjoyable simply to go outside and see what animals are around, there are many easy things you can do to make gardens even more enticing for them. Throughout this book, you'll find ideas for ways to turn an ordinary garden into a thriving wildlife garden.

This tiny mammal is a shrew. Shrews can be attracted to gardens just by letting a patch of wild grasses grow in a quiet corner.

Feathered friends

Birds are found in gardens all year round. No matter where you live, the chances are you'll see birds looking for food or a partner, cleaning themselves, or just resting.

This blackbird's garden visit has been rewarded with a feast of rowan berries.

Common birds

The birds you're most likely to see in gardens, such as sparrows and blue tits, are the types that live there all the time. Others, such as fieldfares, come to gardens at certain times of year but nest elsewhere.

Feeding habits

The main reason that birds visit gardens is to eat and drink. A few – pigeons, for instance – eat anything, but most only like particular things. Look at the shape of a bird's beak for a clue to its diet.

Insect eaters like this wren have long, thin beaks.

Finches have blunt, thick beaks to crack open seeds.

*

Songs and calls

You'll often hear a bird before you see it. Birds make two types of noises: songs and calls. Male birds sing songs in spring to attract a mate and warn away other males. Calls are used by males and females throughout the year to "talk" to other birds.

Green woodpeckers have a laugh-like call. Listen out for them knocking on wood with their beaks, too.

Groups of long-tailed tits make piping "zee zee" calls to let each other know where they are.

Feather care

It's hard for birds to fly with messy feathers, so they need to keep them in tip-top condition. They do this by preening. Watch for birds smoothing the surface of their feathers by sweeping them through their beak.

Most birds, like these gulls, waterproof their feathers with oil from a gland near their tail.

Taking a bath

If a garden has a birdbath in it, or even just a puddle, birds will come to splash in the water. Some also bathe in dust, which removes pests from their feathers. You might even see a bird using ants to keep itself clean.

A mistle thrush sits still while ants eat tiny pests from between its feathers.

Sparrows fluff out their feathers and flap their wings to cover themselves in dust.

Nests and chicks

The breeding season is a busy time for birds. Before they even start the difficult task of raising their young, they must find a mate and build a nest.

Looking for signs

With so much going on throughout the nesting season, it's not hard to see signs of birds raising a family.

Look out and listen for a bird singing in the same place every day. This robin could be attracting a mate, or defending its home.

Many male birds, like the starlings shown here, fight over who owns a nesting area.

*

In the spring, you'll often see birds carrying nesting materials. Magpies use large twigs.

*

Building a nest

Nests come in many shapes and sizes, because each type of bird uses different materials and techniques to build them.

House martins gather mud and use it to build mud cups, which they stick onto ledges and walls.

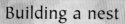

Keeping warm

Birds use their bodies to keep their eggs
warm enough to hatch. Some pluck off
a clump of feathers, leaving an area
of warm skin – a brood patch –
to press against the eggs.

This marsh tit will
warm its eggs with
its bare skin.

Finding food

When the eggs have
hatched, the parents
must work hard to
feed their ever-
hungry babies.
They might fly to
and from the nest
several hundred
times a day with
tidbits to eat.

Baby thrushes open
their mouths wide
to beg for food.

Building supplies

You can encourage birds to
nest in your garden, or help
them to build their nests
elsewhere, by leaving out
nesting materials for them.

All of these things are suitable
nesting materials for birds.

Pet fur

Wool

Hair from
a comb

Feathers

Helping birds

At any time of the year, birds will benefit from a little help to survive. Offering food and shelter will also increase the number of birds that visit your garden.

Feed the birds

Birds need food in every season, but winter and spring are the most important times to help them. It takes all their strength to cope with the cold weather, then raise chicks.

The food you put out in spring gives birds energy to fly around finding small animals to feed to their young.

Giving food

There are lots of ways you can offer food, depending on the size of your garden. The simplest is to leave it on the ground, but this isn't ideal, as it might attract rats. If you have space you could buy a bird table, or if not, a feeder or two.

Robin

Greenfinch

Blackbirds often visit tables, and they also like to hunt for earthworms in flowerbeds.

A handful of seeds quickly attracts birds to the table.

Dunnocks eat seeds that they find on the ground.

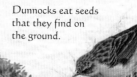

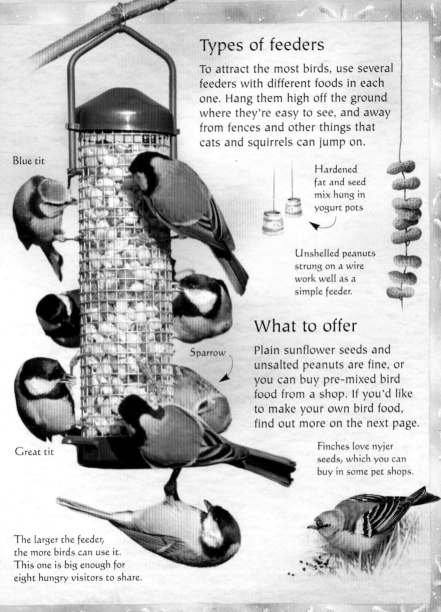

Types of feeders

To attract the most birds, use several feeders with different foods in each one. Hang them high off the ground where they're easy to see, and away from fences and other things that cats and squirrels can jump on.

Blue tit

Hardened fat and seed mix hung in yogurt pots

Unshelled peanuts strung on a wire work well as a simple feeder.

What to offer

Sparrow

Plain sunflower seeds and unsalted peanuts are fine, or you can buy pre-mixed bird food from a shop. If you'd like to make your own bird food, find out more on the next page.

Great tit

Finches love nyjer seeds, which you can buy in some pet shops.

The larger the feeder, the more birds can use it. This one is big enough for eight hungry visitors to share.

A bird cake

This bird cake will not only provide a welcome dinner, it might also attract some rarer types of birds for you to spot.

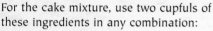

For the cake mixture, use two cupfuls of these ingredients in any combination:
* breadcrumbs * biscuit crumbs
* peanuts * cooked oatmeal
* currants * chopped apple
* sunflower seeds
* raisins * muesli

You will also need:
* cupful of lard * scissors
* empty mesh fruit or nut bags
* string * mixing bowl
* baking tray * saucepan
* wooden spoon

1. Using the spoon, mix all of your ingredients except the lard in the bowl.

2. Melt the lard in the saucepan on a low heat, then slowly pour it into the bowl.

3. Stir the melted lard and dry ingredients together until they're completely mixed.

4. Take handfuls of the mixture and shape it into balls, about the size of your fist. Put them on the tray.

5. Put the tray in the fridge and leave it there until the cakes have set hard. This should take about an hour.

6. Place each ball inside a bag, or tie up the balls with string, and hang them in the garden.

Bird boxes

As winter ends, birds start looking for a place to nest. Try putting up a nest box or two and see if any birds move in. You can buy different kinds that suit particular birds best.

The box in this picture has one side removed, so you can see the nest.

This kind of open-fronted box is used by pied wagtails and flycatchers.

Robins often choose peculiar nesting sites. Leave an old flowerpot in a sheltered spot and they might set up home.

The right place

Bird boxes need to be hung as high as possible, in a quiet area. Don't hang them anywhere that gets lots of direct sunlight, such as a wall that faces south, as too much heat is bad for baby birds.

A tree trunk or an ivy-covered wall is an ideal spot to hang a bird box.

Water for all

Water is just as important for birds – and other animals – as food and shelter. Make sure they have a supply all year round by balancing a bin lid on four bricks and filling it with fresh water each day.

This starling is splashing around to get all its feathers clean.

Creepy crawlies

Even the smallest garden contains hundreds of creepy
crawlies. There are many different types to look
out for, each with its own unique features.

Insects

Most of the tiny creatures you'll see
in a garden are insects. Every insect
has six legs, a pair of antennae, and
usually one or two pairs of wings
(though these might be hard to see).

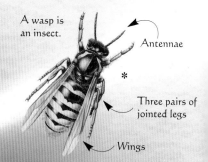

A wasp is
an insect.

Antennae

*

Three pairs of
jointed legs

Wings

Eight-legged creatures

Spiders, harvestmen and mites
all belong to a group of creepy
crawlies with eight legs. They
usually feed on smaller animals,
and a few are poisonous.

This close-up picture of a
spider shows tiny hairs on
its body, which it uses to
sense the world around it.

Most kinds of mites are
very tiny. Red spider mites
like these are easiest to spot
on walls or paving slabs.

Lots of legs

Millipedes and centipedes are types of creepy crawlies with many legs. You'll find them in dark, damp places, such as under bark and in soil, but they don't like light, so they often scurry away when exposed.

Centipedes are hunters. They stab their prey with poisoned claws.

Some snake millipedes have up to 700 legs.

Although "centipede" means "100 legs", they have between 30 and 70.

Long antennae for touching and smelling

Woodlice

Peek under a large stone and you're sure to see woodlice. These belong to a group of animals with hard body armour and more than six legs. They are more closely related to crabs than insects.

A woodlouse's body armour is made of overlapping sections.

Woodlice grow by shedding their hard coverings.

Pill bugs are a type of woodlouse that can roll into a tight ball.

Which is which?

It can be hard to tell some types of creepy crawlies apart. If you spot a tiny creature, notice its markings, the number of legs, whether it has wings, and how it behaves. A field guide will help you to identify it.

Water boatmen are insects, but some of their six legs are hard to see.

Its eight legs tell you that this harvestman is related to spiders.

Insect world

Insects are intriguing and complex creatures. They often look and behave differently at each stage of their lives, so watch out for both adults and babies in gardens.

Laying eggs

Almost all insects make babies by pairing up with a mate. After this, the female lays eggs. She usually chooses a safe spot on or near something that the young insects can eat when they hatch.

Lacewing eggs have stalks attached, to keep hungry ants from reaching them.

A potter wasp's young hatch from eggs in clay "pots". They are fed on caterpillars.

Growth and change

Many insects start off as babies called larvae. For most of their lives larvae look nothing like their parents, but when they reach a certain age they transform inside cocoons called pupae. You might see these on trees, fences and walls.

Meadow brown butterfly

1. Like most insects, adult butterflies lay eggs. *

2. An egg hatches into a caterpillar, which eats as much as it can. *

3. The caterpillar's skin hardens and becomes a pupa. *

4. Inside the pupa, the caterpillar's body changes. It emerges as a butterfly. *

Mini adults

Insects such as dragonflies hatch from their eggs already looking like miniature adults. At this stage the young are called nymphs. A nymph grows by shedding its skin from time to time until it reaches full size. Look for dragonflies and old skins if there's a pond nearby.

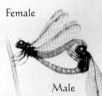

Female

Male

1. These dragonflies are mating. Next, the female will lay her eggs.

Old skin

2. Each egg hatches into a nymph. It spends two years growing and shedding its skin.

This dragonfly nymph has climbed out of its skin to become an adult.

Insect parents

Insects usually look after their eggs until they hatch. Some even take care of their young after that, too. Others, such as moths and butterflies, abandon the eggs after they are laid.

If you get too near an earwig's eggs, their mother will snap her pincers at you.

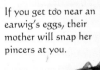

Hidden babies

Some young insects are harder to spot than others. Froghopper nymphs, for instance, are hidden inside blobs of foam on plant stems.

Adult froghopper

Close-up of young froghopper

The foam is sometimes called cuckoo spit.

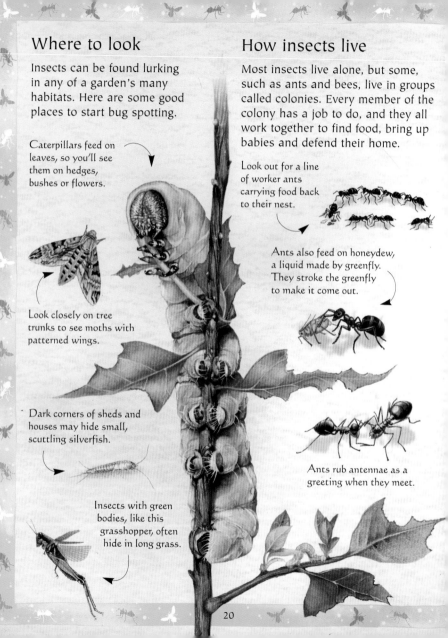

Where to look

Insects can be found lurking in any of a garden's many habitats. Here are some good places to start bug spotting.

Caterpillars feed on leaves, so you'll see them on hedges, bushes or flowers.

Look closely on tree trunks to see moths with patterned wings.

Dark corners of sheds and houses may hide small, scuttling silverfish.

Insects with green bodies, like this grasshopper, often hide in long grass.

How insects live

Most insects live alone, but some, such as ants and bees, live in groups called colonies. Every member of the colony has a job to do, and they all work together to find food, bring up babies and defend their home.

Look out for a line of worker ants carrying food back to their nest.

Ants also feed on honeydew, a liquid made by greenfly. They stroke the greenfly to make it come out.

Ants rub antennae as a greeting when they meet.

A garden buffet

Almost everything in a garden is food for one insect or another. This includes leaves, plant roots, rubbish, animals' blood, dung and even other insects.

Wasps eat sweet things like this spilled marmalade.

Robber flies act like vampires, pouncing on their victims and sucking out their juices.

Self-defence

All insects face the threat of big, hungry enemies, but many have clever ways of hiding or protecting themselves. See how many you can spot.

*

Enemies think this hoverfly is a wasp, but it's really a harmless lookalike.

Hungry animals mistake the shapes on an eyed hawkmoth's wings for a scary enemy's eyes.

*

*

This comma butterfly is well disguised among dead leaves.

Useful insects

As well as being food for many other creatures, insects are important for other reasons too. Some of the vital things they do include burying the bodies of dead animals and helping plants to make seeds.

Burying beetles bury dead animals by digging earth from beneath them. They feed on the bodies.

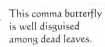

Pollen carriers

Most garden flowers produce a powder called pollen, which is carried around by insects. Without this help, flowers couldn't make seeds to grow into new plants.

A sweet treat

Insects visit flowers to drink a sweet liquid called nectar. As they seek their prize, pollen sticks to their bodies. The insects carry it to other flowers of the same kind, which can then make fruits with seeds inside.

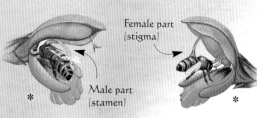

Female part (stigma)

Male part (stamen)

*

Pollen rubs off a flower's male part onto the bee's body as it drinks nectar.

*

When the insect visits another flower, the pollen sticks to its female part.

Busy bees

A bee spends its whole day buzzing from flower to flower, drinking nectar and gathering pollen. If you watch a bee on its trips, you'll see it only visits one sort of flower at a time.

This honey bee is picking up pollen grains as it clambers over flowers.

Moths

Moths mostly drink nectar at night. Their sensitive antennae can detect a flower's delicious scent in the dark.

You can identify a moth by its feathery antennae.

Butterflies

Butterflies feed on nothing but nectar during their short adult lives. Most of them only survive long enough to mate and lay eggs, sometimes less than a week.

This swallowtail butterfly is drinking nectar from a lavender flower.

Drinking tubes

Most pollen carriers have a mouthpart called a proboscis, which sucks up nectar like a drinking straw. Butterflies and moths unfurl their long mouthparts to reach into flowers.

A butterfly's proboscis curls up when it's not being used.

Other pollen carriers

A few types of flies, beetles and wasps also feed on nectar. Most of them have fairly short mouthparts, so they tend to feed on flat, open flowers where the nectar is easy to reach.

Look out for wasps, beetles and flies on flowers with a flattish shape.

Wasp on Michaelmas daisy

Dronefly on hogweed

Web weavers

Spiders look a bit like insects, but they are actually creatures called arachnids. Spiders are helpful garden visitors, because they eat bugs that harm plants.

Wonderful webs

The most well-known feature of spiders is their ability to spin delicate, silky webs. These act as traps to catch the insects they feed on. Webs are easiest to see when they're wet, so look for them after rain, or early on a dewy morning.

A garden spider can spin an intricate orb web like this one in about an hour.

House spiders spin sheet webs (also called cobwebs) in corners.

Wall spiders spin tube-like webs in cracks in walls. Bugs fall inside.

Webless spiders

Not all spiders spin webs to catch food. Some attack their prey directly by pouncing and grabbing.

Crab spiders can run sideways like a crab. They seize insects with their front legs.

Caught in a trap

You won't always see spiders on their webs – they usually hide nearby. When an insect becomes snagged, the spider rushes out to stab it with its deadly fangs.

Sometimes, you might see a spider binding an insect in threads before eating it.

A dangerous date

Female garden spiders are bigger than males, and more vicious. When a male approaches a female to mate, he spins an escape thread so he can get away quickly if she attacks. He may have to approach her many times before she allows him to mate.

Escape thread

Male garden spider

Female garden spider

Mother spiders

Female spiders are good parents. Some mother spiders hide their eggs to keep them safe, but others wrap them up and take them wherever they go.

This wolf spider is carrying her eggs in a ball of protective web threads.

Slugs and snails

Unlike other kinds of creepy crawlies, slugs and snails have no legs at all. They creep around slowly on a slick of slime, looking for plants to nibble.

Spot the difference

Snails and slugs are alike in many ways, but it's easy to tell them apart. Snails have hard shells on their backs, and almost all slugs don't.

Snails and slugs have one pair of tentacles for seeing and a smaller pair for touching. *

Grey slug

Snails and slugs leave behind a silvery trail of slime wherever they go.

The snail trail

During the day, snails and slugs cluster together in damp, sheltered spots. At night or after rain, they go out to feed, usually returning afterwards to where they started. Find these meeting places by following the shiny trails the slimy creatures left behind.

You can see the slime glistening on this snail's body.

Rasping tongues

Snails and slugs eat both fresh and rotting leaves, sometimes doing a lot of damage to garden plants. They feed using rows of tiny saw-like teeth on their tongue. Listen to one closely and you might be able to hear its tongue rasping.

Look for holes left behind in plants after slugs have finished eating.

Safety first

A snail can retreat into its shell when threatened, or if the weather is too cold or dry. Slugs burrow into the soil to keep their bodies moist, or repel enemies by curling up and making thick, nasty-tasting goo.

Black slug

Slugs squish their bodies into a ball if something tries to harm them.

Snails can seal up their shell with a plug of dried mucus.

Male and female

In spring and summer, you might see a pair of snails coming together to make eggs. They crawl over each other for several hours before starting to mate.

Brown-lipped snails preparing to mate

*

Usually, female animals lay eggs, but a snail is both male and female. After mating, both partners lay many eggs in the soil. These hatch into tiny snails a few weeks later.

Snail eggs look like pale balls.

*

Water babies

Even a tiny garden pond is home to many animals, including bugs, snails, and amphibians such as frogs. Amphibians have their babies in water, so ponds are vital to their survival.

Fascinating frogs

Like all amphibians, frogs are born in water but spend time on land, too. During winter, many avoid the cold by sleeping in mud on the pond bottom. In spring, the water comes alive with frisky frogs looking for a partner.

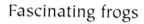

Frogs catch bugs with their sticky tongues.

Long back legs for jumping

This frog is puffing up its throat to croak. The sound attracts a mate.

Warts and all

Toads are very similar to frogs, but with dumpier bodies and dry, warty skin. You're not likely to see a toad during the day, as they tend to hide in burrows and under rocks.

People used to think that touching a toad gave you warts.

A toad has shorter back legs than a frog.

Newts

Newts are a type of amphibian with a long tail and smooth skin. The best time to see them in garden ponds is between April and June, when they breed.

Female smooth newts have dull brown bodies.

Males have patterned bodies and crests on their tails.

Having babies

Amphibians' eggs are called spawn. Frogspawn comes in big, wobbly clumps, whereas toadspawn is laid in long strings. Look for spawn in shallow areas of a pond. Each egg hatches into a baby called a tadpole, which looks very different from its parents.

These pictures show how much a tadpole changes as it grows into a frog.

Newts lay their eggs individually on pond plants.

A young newt has tiny legs, and feathery gills for breathing.

Tadpole at 1 week old

8 weeks old

11 weeks old

Adult frog

A ribbon of toadspawn can be up to 2m (6.5ft) long.

This frog is surrounded by its spawn. The black blobs will become tadpoles.

A wildlife pond

Natural ponds and pools are becoming more rare, but a garden pond offers animals water to drink or live in instead.

Making a pond

If you want to create a simple wildlife pond, you'll need pond liner, rocks and a square metre or so of space.

Dig your pond in a sunny spot away from trees, so fallen leaves won't make the water dirty.

Spring is the best time of year for pond-making.

Dig the shelf about 15cm (6in) down.

1. Dig a hole about 60cm (24in) deep, 70cm (28in) wide and 1m (40in) long, with gently sloping sides.

2. Dig a shallow shelf all around the side of the hole, so animals can climb in and out.

3. Completely cover the sides and bottom of the hole with sheets of newspaper.

You can buy pond liner at a garden centre.

Cover the exposed liner between the rocks with soil.

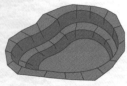

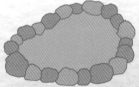

4. Line the pond with liner, leaving about 20cm (8in) extra all around the edge.

5. Use stones to weigh down the extra liner all around the hole.

6. Fill the pond with tapwater from a hose, or rainwater from a water butt.

Choosing plants

The most important things to put in a new pond are plants – a mix of floating types to create shade for creatures under the water, and waterweeds to give them oxygen. Some plants spread very fast, so you might need to remove a few now and again.

Shallow-water flowers can stand on the pond's shelf in pots, or you can pin their roots down with stones.

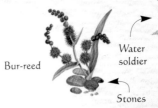

Water soldier

Bur-reed

Stones

These plants attach themselves to the pond bottom by long stems.

The leaves of these plants float on the water's surface.

Broad-leaved pondweed

Water lily

*

Water crowfoot

Frogbit

Algae are microscopic plants which appear by themselves in all ponds.

Pond animals

There's no need to buy any animals to put in a pond. Simply add the plants and wait for the local wildlife to move in.

All kinds of animals will want to visit a new pond, including thirsty birds like this goldfinch.

Fish

Some people like to put fish in their garden ponds. It's better not to, though, as they eat tadpoles and frogspawn, as well as the bugs and plants that wild garden visitors feed on.

Pond insects

Ponds are home to hundreds of insects. Some, such as dragonflies, start their lives in the water, then leave when they're fully grown and return as adults to lay eggs. Others spend their whole lives there.

A big pond might attract herons, which eat both fish and frogs.

*

This spectacular emperor dragonfly is shown life-sized.

Look for pond skaters walking on the water.

Other pond life

Some animals that you can see on land, such as spiders and snails, have relatives that live in ponds. Look for them on pond plants, both above and below the water's surface.

Tiny creatures

Ponds are teeming with animals that are almost too small to see. Larger animals feed on them.

In real life, these water fleas are barely bigger than a pinhead.

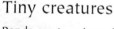

Water spiders live under water. They make a "tent" from a bubble of air.

Ramshorn snails lay their eggs on pond plants.

A mini marsh

Many pond creatures also thrive in marshy areas. To make one, dig a hole about 10cm (4in) deep and 40cm (16in) wide and line it with pond liner. Fill it with water, then add some soil to create a shallow mudpool.

These flowers will grow well in a marsh.

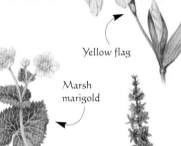

Yellow flag

Grass snakes might visit your marsh. Don't worry, they're harmless to people.

Marsh marigold

*

Purple loosestrife

Stone shelters

Toads and frogs need dark places to hide when they're not in the water. The best sort of shelter is a rockery made of large, flattish stones or bricks, piled up loosely so the animals can wriggle beneath. Lizards and snakes might rest there, too.

Slow worms like to hide under rocks. They're actually a type of lizard.

*

The stones on the right are surrounded by heather. Planting rockery flowers attracts bugs for larger animals to eat.

Purple aubretia

Starry saxifrage

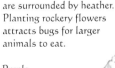

Under the ground

Even the parts of a garden you can't see are full of life. Animals make their homes and search for food under the ground, just as they do in the world above.

Underground nurseries

Many insects lay their eggs in soil. When the larvae hatch out, they feed on plant roots. Several years might pass before you see them on the surface as adults.

A cranefly's larva is called a leatherjacket.

Cranefly

Moth caterpillars grow in cocoons.

Dot moth

Beetle larvae are also known as grubs.

Cockchafer beetle

Worms

Worms live in underground burrows. They swallow soil and pass it back out of their bodies just below the ground. This soil contains chemicals from deeper down, which are good for plants.

Some worms leave behind squiggly piles of dirt called casts on the ground.

Worms often sleep through the summer in their burrows.

A worm grips the sides of its burrow with tiny bristles on its body.

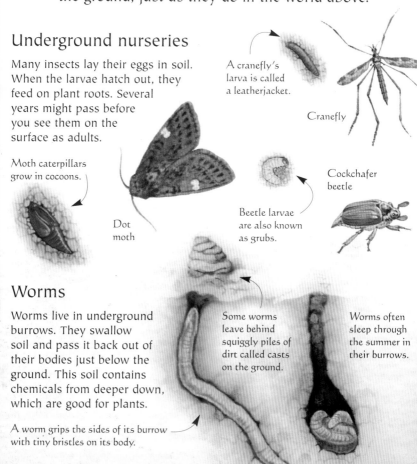

Worm watching

Worms are important garden animals because they keep the soil rich by churning it up. You can make this simple wormery to see how.

You will need:
* a large jar * fine sand
* soil * paper * string
* a cluster of leaves
* some earthworms

Tie the paper in place with the string.

Return the worms to the garden afterwards.

1. Put alternating layers of sand and soil in the jar. Place the leaves on top, as food for the worms.

2. Dig up some worms and put them in the jar. Wrap paper around it to keep out light.

3. After two days, remove the paper. See how the worms have mixed up the layers.

Digging machines

Moles spend most of their time digging tunnels and hunting for worms. When they come to the surface it's usually to find a mate, or to hunt for food on a damp night. Telltale mounds of earth called molehills show where they've been.

Moles have long, sharp claws for digging, and sensitive noses for sniffing out food.

Night-time

When you go to sleep, some animals are only just waking up. Most come out at dusk, but others emerge later and stay up until dawn.

The night shift

You'd be surprised at the number and variety of creatures that lurk in your garden in the dark. If you go out with a torch, here are some of the things you might see. Be as quiet as you can.

Green lacewings rest on trees and bushes.

Beetles fly around, attracted to lights.

Male dark bush crickets chirp loudly on summer evenings.

Wood mice come out in the dark to climb bushes and feed on their berries.

Female glow-worms light up their bodies to attract males. They are very rare garden visitors.

This tawny owl is swooping down to catch a mouse in its razor-sharp claws.

Owls

Owls are meat eaters. They hunt for mice and other small animals, and may even attack other birds. Owls fly almost silently, but you might hear them make a "hoo hoo" call while they are resting in trees.

Bats

Bats can often be seen at dusk, swooping over gardens to catch flying bugs. They sleep through winter, so you're most likely to see them in the warmer months.

The pipistrelle is the most common garden bat. Its body is small enough to fit in a matchbox.

Late bloomers

If you plant a mixture of night-blooming flowers like the ones shown here, they will attract lots of different moths. These, in turn, will attract hungry bats.

Honeysuckle and evening primrose are night-blooming flowers that are often visited by moths.

Furry creatures

Badgers, mice and other furry creatures come to gardens to feed. You're less likely to see them than birds or bugs, though, as they are shy around people.

Badgers

Badgers are most likely to come to gardens in the countryside. They snuffle around looking for earthworms, often digging up flowerbeds as they go.

*

You can recognize a badger by its stripy face.

Foxes

Foxes used to be only countryside animals, but the loss of their natural habitat has led them to towns and cities too. You might see one running across a road, or sniffing around bins at twilight for scraps to eat.

This type of fox, called a red fox, is the only one you're likely to see in a garden.

Mice and rats

Mice and rats eat almost anything, and will move into your house if they get the chance. It's best not to drive them away completely, because they're eaten by owls, but don't encourage them. Keep the ground clear of food scraps from bins and bird feeders.

* Yellow-necked mice usually live in woods, but visit gardens too.

Brown rats often hide under sheds, coming out at dusk to feed. *

House mice sometimes nest in secret corners of houses and sheds. *

Shrews

Shrews are mouse-sized animals with tiny, sharp teeth for biting into creepy crawlies. A shrew must eat its own body weight in food every day to survive.

Shrews come out at night to hunt for slugs and worms. In the daytime they hide under plants.

Don't feed the animals

Although it's tempting to attract foxes and badgers to a garden by leaving out food, it's better not to. Feeding these animals makes them too dependent on people, so leave them to scavenge or hunt for themselves.

Foxes are good hunters. They kill small animals by rearing up and stamping on them.

A winter rest

Winter is the toughest season for wildlife. Food is scarce, and temperatures are low. At this time of year, animals need your help the most.

A big sleep

Sleeping through the winter is called hibernation. Most hibernating animals hide away in a shelter, such as a burrow or a hollow log. If you find a hibernating animal, leave it in peace.

Pipistrelle bats huddle up in old trees, or even in people's attics.

Hedgehogs curl up and sleep in leaf piles.

The hunt for food

Hibernating animals eat lots before they sleep, to avoid starving during winter. Many other animals face a struggle to find food in the cold.

A well-stocked feeder could be a hungry bird's ticket to survival.

Snack storage

Some animals survive winter by planning ahead. Squirrels, for instance, hide nuts in autumn to dig up and eat in winter.

A squirrel can sniff out buried nuts when it needs a meal.

Sun seekers

Another way that animals can deal with the cold is to go to a warmer country. When the seasons change again, they travel all the way back to where they started.

Swift

Watch for these birds arriving in the summer.

Swallow

*

Winter bugs

Many bugs spend winter sleeping in pupae or plant stems. But some, such as spiders, aren't affected by the cold. You'll see them going about their business as normal.

Bark beetles hibernate in tree bark, or under dead leaves.

A spider's body contains chemicals that act as natural antifreeze.

Most butterflies and moths spend winter safe inside a pupa.

A bug hotel

You can offer hibernating insects a safe place to stay by making this simple bug hotel.

Canes or straws of varying widths will attract different bugs.

You will need:
⁕ a bunch of hollow garden canes or drinking straws ⁕ string

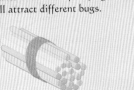

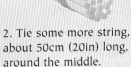

1. Tie the straws or canes together in the middle with string.

2. Tie some more string, about 50cm (20in) long, around the middle.

3. Attach the bug hotel to a tree branch and wait for your guests to arrive.

Wildlife detectives

Garden visitors can be hard to spot. You'll never see every single creature that comes to a garden, but you might be able to find proof that they were there.

Plant clues

Leaves often reveal a lot about a visitor's activities. Leaf-cutter bees, for instance, tear up rose leaves to make nests for their eggs. Some insect larvae eat leaves from the inside, leaving trail-like marks as they go.

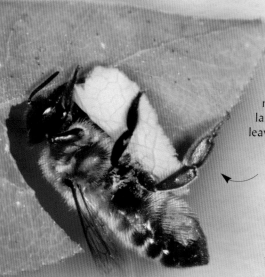

When this leaf-cutter bee has finished, a crescent-shaped hole will be left behind.

The blotches on these leaves, called leaf mines, are tunnels left by hungry larvae.

Footprints

Animals leave distinctive tracks in soft mud or snow. If you're really keen to see tracks, try putting out a shallow tray of sand overnight and see if anything walks through it.

Fore (front) foot	Hind (back) foot	
	*	A fox makes neat, dog-like prints in a straight line.
Fore foot	Hind foot *	A badger's wide prints show five toes with sharp claws.
Fore foot	Hind foot *	Cat prints show no claw marks.

Feeding signs

Nibbled pine cones and nuts are a sure sign that something has had a meal in a garden. Look out for empty nut shells on the ground beneath trees, or even stored in cracks in the bark. Cones are more common if there are pine trees nearby. Most animal species tackle their food differently, so check for teeth or beak marks.

Squirrels remove the scales completely from a pine cone, leaving a rough-looking stem.

A woodpecker shreds the scales to reach the seeds inside.

Spotted woodpeckers sometimes wedge cones in tree bark to shred them.

A squirrel has split this hazelnut shell at the top, and gnawed it near the base.

A blue tit chipped away this walnut's shell to reach the tasty treat inside.

A hawfinch cracked this cherry stone in half. Many seed-eating birds do this.

Telltale droppings

You might be able to identify a visitor from the shape and colour of its droppings, where they're found, or even what they contain.

Hedgehog droppings are black, and often contain shiny insect remains.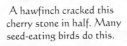

Badger droppings are about 10cm (4in) long. They're left in specially-dug holes.

Bird clues

The clues that birds leave in a garden are different from those of any other animal. Here are some things to spot.

Empty nests

In the autumn, when their babies have flown away, birds leave their nests empty. Try looking for one in a tree or hedge, or on a wall.

Long-tailed tits make egg-shaped nests in brambles or gorse.

Song thrushes build bowl-like nests in hedges.

The snail's enemy

In dry weather, earthworms are scarce, so song thrushes eat snails instead. They hammer the shells against a stone to break them open. Look out for bits of shell left near a stone.

This song thrush is breaking a snail shell on its stone, or "anvil".

Pellets in pieces

Many birds swallow food whole, then cough up the solid remains as a pellet. Use rubber gloves and tweezers to take apart any pellets you find and discover what's inside.

Crow pellets contain small stones and plant or insect parts.

Gulls eat almost anything. This herring gull pellet contains foil, bones, plastic and string.

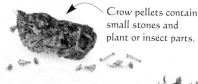

Feathers

Birds' feathers are usually easy to find, because their owners shed them at least once every year. Feathers come in many sizes and shapes depending on the job they do.

Blue tit

Long primary feathers are used for flying.

Contour feathers cover the body, giving it a smooth, sleek surface.

Fluffy down feathers grow next to the skin. They keep the bird warm.

Fancy feathers

Some birds have very distinctive feathers. If you find a feather, you can use its shape and pattern to help you identify its owner in a bird book.

Short feathers like this grow near the base of the wing. This one came from a jay.

*

A mallard's feather seems to change colour when held up to the light.

*

You might find a pheasant's stripy tail feather in a garden in the countryside.

*

Surprising visitors

Sometimes, you might see unexpected animals in a garden. Most come from nearby habitats, but others could be stopping to take a rest on a long journey.

Local wildlife

The types of animals found in a garden depend on where it is. So if you live near, say, a moor, you'll see different garden visitors from someone living near the coast.

Near woodland

A wood full of mature trees makes a perfect habitat for many kinds of animals. Rare bats, birds, butterflies and deer might pay gardens a visit if there is woodland nearby.

Long-eared bat

*

*

Speckled wood butterfly

Roe deer are timid, but they occasionally venture into gardens near to woodlands.

Near heathland

Reptiles are normally hard to find in gardens, but if you're near a heath you stand a much better chance of seeing one.

Common adders are poisonous. They rarely hurt people, though.

Near water

Water always attracts living things, so in a garden near the sea, a river or a marsh you'll see an even wider selection of animals and plants.

Yellow wagtails live near to rivers inland, and by salt marshes near the sea.

Sand wasps live in nests on beaches.

Burnet rose is a common wild flower around the coast.

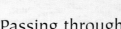

Near fields

Fields are home to many small mammals, which will sometimes visit gardens to search for food.

Weasels hunt for birds, insects and other mammals.

Rabbits

Passing through

Some types of birds make trips to other countries each year, to find food and raise a family. If they stop to rest, or get blown off course, they could end up in a garden.

Whinchats spend winter in Africa, but they're very occasionally seen in British gardens during summer.

In the treetops

Trees are the largest flowering plants on Earth. They offer many things to wildlife: safe spots to make a home, shade from the sun, and plenty of things to eat.

Branches

Birds often nest in the branches of trees, or use them as perches. Squirrels also build their leafy nests where the branches join the trunk.

Grey squirrels like this one are expert climbers and acrobats, using their tails to balance and their claws to grip.

Leaves

Leaves are very important to a tree, as they make food that keeps it alive. They also act as handy places for insects to rest or lay their eggs.

The swellings on this leaf are called galls. They're made by various bugs laying eggs inside it.

Cherry galls

Spangle galls

Kidney galls

Bug-filled bark

A tree's trunk is covered in hard bark. As some types of bark get older they develop cracks, where creepy crawlies set up home.

A treecreeper probes cracks in tree bark to find bugs to eat.

Springtime blossom

In spring, trees burst into flower. Some types of blossom contain sweet nectar, which insects drink. Look for bees and wasps flying from tree to tree to sip nectar.

Apple blossom's aroma attracts bees and other pollen carriers.

Fruits and seeds

After pollen carriers have visited a tree flower, it develops into a fruit with seeds inside. Fruits are eaten by birds, which carry away the seeds in their bodies or drop them on the ground.

Cherries are eaten by bugs and birds in summer.

Jays eat acorns, the fruit of oak trees.

Blackthorn berries, called sloes, grow in the autumn.

Holly berries are an important winter wildlife food.

Trees for tomorrow

Even a single tree in a garden is enormously helpful to wildlife. It takes many years for a young tree to grow, but if you have the chance to plant one today you'll be helping the wildlife of the future.

A single tree, such as this beech, can be home to furry animals, birds and hundreds of bugs.

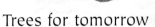

Gardening for wildlife

Almost every flower or bush is useful to wildlife, although some types are better than others. The best kind of wildlife garden has plants of many sizes, shapes and species.

Local plants

Wildlife tends to be most attracted to native plants, which come from the country where you live. These grow more easily than non-natives, because the local soil and climate suit them better.

All of these flowers are native to Britain.

The wild side

Most native flowers are what people call wild flowers – types that spread naturally without being planted. You can buy seeds if you want to grow particular kinds, though.

Field poppy

Teasel

St John's wort

Ox-eye daisy

Just for show

Many kinds of flowers on sale in garden centres and shops are ornamental varieties. These have been specially bred to look good, but over time, they have lost many of their natural features. Most have no nectar or scent, and some don't even make pollen, so they're not very useful to wildlife.

Mix it up

Don't worry if you have a lot of non-native flowers in your garden. It's fine to have them too, as some kinds are useful to wildlife. The most important thing is variety.

These non-natives are good for a wildlife garden.

A foxglove's pattern of spots guides bees to the nectar inside.

Insects visit sunflowers for their nectar, and birds eat their seeds.

Forget-me-not

Cranesbill

Shrubs and bushes

Animals need large plants as well as flowers. If your garden is too small for a native tree, shrubs and bushes provide lots of the same benefits but in a compact form.

Many bird species nest in elder bushes or feed on their berries.

The fruits of this guelder rose bush have attracted a hungry mouse.

Its plump fruits make cotoneaster a great shrub for wildlife.

A butterfly garden

On a summer's day, you're likely to see butterflies
flitting around in gardens. You can attract more by
growing some of the flowers shown here.

Seasonal selections

Butterflies are out and about
from mid March until late
September, so a mix of spring,
summer and autumn blooming
flowers will keep them coming
for as long as possible.

Peacock butterflies
are active all summer,
when these hemp
agrimony flowers bloom.

Colour counts

Every type of pollen carrier has
favourite flower colours. Butterflies
are especially attracted to flowers
with purple, pink or white petals.

Brimstone butterfly
on aubretia flowers

Buddleias are so popular
with butterflies that
they're sometimes referred
to as butterfly bushes.

52

What shape?

Generally, butterflies choose small, tube-shaped flowers that they can stand on while they drink nectar. They also visit daisy-like flowers with tiny parts in the middle.

Small copper on Michaelmas daisy

Red admiral on ice plant

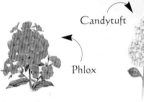

The flowers shown below are appealing to butterflies, too.

Green-veined white on wallflower

Candytuft

Phlox

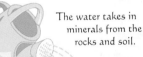

A butterfly puddle

As well as nectar, butterflies need water to stay alive. Some also need chemicals called minerals, which they get from mud puddles. Create a puddle and groups of butterflies might come to rest and drink.

The water takes in minerals from the rocks and soil.

Top up the water from time to time.

1. Bury a large flowerpot all the way up to the rim.

2. Fill it almost to the top with gravel, rocks and a little soil.

3. Add water until a natural puddle forms at the top.

Going wild

Many people work hard to keep their gardens tidy and weed-free, but wildlife thrives in messy areas. If you can, let a corner of your garden grow wild to attract more wildlife.

Rye grass

A mini meadow

Create a mini wildlife meadow by letting a patch of grass grow long, with a few native grasses like the ones shown here. Bugs and small animals live in long grass, and larger animals hunt them.

*

You might occasionally see a kestrel looking for mice in your meadow.

Annual meadow grass

What is a weed?

Some people say weeds are bad, but others say they're good plants that are growing in the wrong place. It's certainly true that many plants that are described as weeds are helpful to wildlife.

A patch of nettles in the corner of a garden offers butterflies a place to lay eggs.

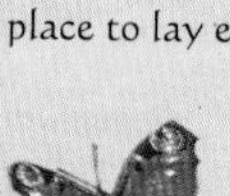

Brambles provide animals with shelter and tasty berries.

Peacock butterfly

Dandelions attract bees, and some types of birds too.

Weed control

You need to be careful when growing weeds, as they can spread quickly and even harm other plants. Try not to let any grow outside your wild area.

Goose grass is sticky, smelly and not much use to wildlife, so keep it out of the garden.

Wood piles

Old tree branches, logs and dead leaves needn't be burned or thrown away. Put them in a pile where they won't be disturbed, and they might become home to bugs, slimy creatures, or even a hibernating hedgehog.

Stag beetles lay eggs in rotten wood piles. The larvae live there for many years.

A fruity feast

If you have a fruit tree, don't clear away the ripe fruits that fall from it in autumn. A few left on the lawn will soon be eaten by bugs, birds or mammals such as foxes.

This wasp is sucking the sweet juices from a fallen plum.

Harmony with nature

"Organic" is a word which describes living things.
Organic gardens rely on nature rather than man-made
chemicals to grow well, so they're good for wildlife.

Healthy soil

Certain plants, such as beans, sweet peas and
lupins, turn nitrogen from the air into food for
soil. Growing them helps to keep soil and other
plants healthy. You can also feed garden soil
with compost, a rich mixture of rotting waste,
instead of man-made chemical plant foods.
(There's more about compost on pages 58-59.)

Plants like
this sweet pea
are both pretty and
good for gardens.

Natural pest control

All gardeners want to protect their
plants from pests and disease,
and many use pesticides to do
this. Nature has its own
solution, though, in the
shape of other garden
animals that will eat pests.
Encourage them to live in
your garden, if you can.

Greenfly are notorious garden
pests, but they're no match
for this hungry ladybird.

Helper plants

You can keep plants healthy with the help of another plant. The helper will either repel pests or attract the animals that eat them. Blackfly, for instance, eat tomato plants. But planting French marigolds between the tomato plants gets rid of the blackfly, which don't like the marigolds' scent.

Marigolds repel many types of garden pests.

Rosemary

These strong-smelling herbs are helper plants.

Garlic

A hands-on approach

A good wildlife garden needs a certain number of weeds, but they can take over if you let them. Digging them up by hand is safer for animals and the soil than using weedkiller.

Bindweed is a harmful weed, because it spreads far and fast. Pull it out whenever you see it.

Not all bad

Before you declare war on all the unwanted plants and animals in the garden, remember that everything has some role to play in nature. Although they're a nuisance to you, they could be a vital meal to a starving animal.

Today's plant-chewing caterpillar is tomorrow's pollen-carrying butterfly.

Slugs destroy garden plants, but they're also dinner for hungry hedgehogs.

Soil food

Compost is a mixture of natural things, such as dead plants, which are slowly rotting. A compost heap may not be pretty, but it has many benefits for your garden.

Natural recycling

Plants and animals are still full of useful chemicals after they die. The natural process of decay, helped by living things such as worms, allows these chemicals to be set free. This is what happens in a compost heap.

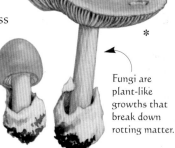

* Fungi are plant-like growths that break down rotting matter.

* Earthworms help to turn rotted matter into a useful mixture.

Why make compost?

Mixing compost with your soil makes it richer, helping plants to grow well without needing artificial plant food. Keeping a compost heap is also a good way to use things which would normally be thrown away, such as kitchen waste. There are lots of things you can add to a heap.

Plant matter such as vegetables and leaves is good for compost. You can also use grass clippings or old teabags.

Don't add meat scraps – they encourage rats.

Caring for your heap

You can keep compost in a pile, but it's better to use a container such as a dustbin, with holes in the bottom for drainage. This helps it to stay warm and rot more quickly. To keep the compost healthy and stop it from smelling, you need to water it and turn it over with a garden fork from time to time.

The simplest compost heap is a pile of rotting things in a corner of the garden.

Compost community

Compost is not only excellent soil food, it's also a magnet for wildlife. Shortly after you start a compost heap, you'll see lots of living things start to move in.

House crickets lay their eggs on compost and rubbish heaps.

The Devil's coach-horse is one of many types of beetles that live in compost.

Amphibians such as this toad are drawn to the warmth and damp of compost, as well as its tasty worms.

Wildlife in danger

Many wild animals are struggling to survive. People harm their food supplies and destroy the safe places where they breed, but there are things you can do to protect them.

Alien invaders

Some native animals are threatened by non-native (alien) species, which are fiercer, or better able to survive. Grey squirrels, for instance, compete with their red relatives for food and breeding places. If red squirrels live in your area, you could help them by buying a squirrel feeder which greys are too heavy to use.

American grey squirrels carry a disease which is lethal to the UK's native reds.

Because of grey squirrels, red squirrels like this might one day die out in Britain.

Problem plants

Although some non-native plants are good for wildlife, a few types can damage the natural balance. They take water and space from native plants and may even breed with them, creating a hybrid – a new plant that's a mix of the two. Sometimes, the hybrids replace the natives.

Wild bluebells like these are under threat from Spanish varieties.

No place to go

Huge numbers of natural habitats, such as moors, are being replaced by farmland and houses. As a result, frogs, hedgehogs and many insects are being squeezed out of the wild. In some cases, gardens are their only hope.

*

Over half of the UK's 60 native butterfly species are threatened by a lack of overgrown land.

Comma butterfly

High brown fritillary

Poison peril

Poison is a serious problem for many animals. Farmers often spray crops with chemicals to destroy pests, but this affects the animals that feed on them too. They are left with nothing to eat, or even killed by eating the poisoned bugs.

The more insects are poisoned, the fewer will be left for insect-eating birds such as swallows.

Hazards at home

Even in a garden, animals can find themselves in danger. Prowling pets, weedkiller, slug pellets and garden bonfires are all potential hazards for local wildlife.

Cats kill garden birds. A pet cat should be fitted with a collar and bell, so birds can hear it coming.

Always check wood and leaf piles for sleeping hedgehogs before lighting a bonfire.

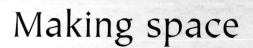

Making space

If you have very little space in your garden, or no garden at all, there are still quick and easy things you can do for wildlife.

Sink and swim

An old enamel sink, cat litter tray or similar container can easily become a mini wildlife pond. Just place it in a sunny spot and fill it with water. Add a few stones, so animals can climb in and out easily.

If you have room, add a small water plant or two, such as this starwort.

Stones

Butterflies might come to rest on an ivy-covered wall in the sun.

Climbing plants

You can use house or garden walls to grow climbing plants such as ivy. These provide wildlife with berries in winter and shelter all year round.

A hidey-hole

A piece of wood or corrugated iron propped up against the side of a shed or wall might be all you need to make a welcome hidey-hole for small animals. Make sure the iron has no sharp corners or edges.

Small animals, such as toads, tend to shelter in the shadows beneath things.

Plants in pots

If you haven't much ground for planting, you could grow things in pots instead. A small shrub or a few flowers and herbs will attract more visitors than you might think.

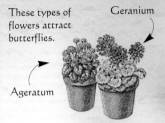

These types of flowers attract butterflies.

Ageratum

Geranium

Bees are attracted by the smell of catmint.

A window box

Even without a garden, it's still possible to help garden wildlife. Window boxes or glass-mounted bird feeders don't need any ground at all.

Plants like these in a window box will attract pollen carriers.

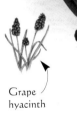

Snowdrop

Crocus

Grape hyacinth

Get involved

Another way to help wildlife is to join a local conservation group. You can find contact details for some groups on the Usborne Quicklinks Website at www.usborne-quicklinks.com.

This feeder has suction cups so you can stick it to a window. It's an ideal way to see birds close up.

INDEX

ACKNOWLEDGEMENTS
Managing designer: Karen Tomlins
Cover design: Joanne Kirkby
Artwork co-ordinator: Louise Breen
Website advisor: Lisa Watts

PHOTO CREDITS (t = top, m = middle, b = bottom, l = left, r = right)
1 Jean Michel Labat/Ardea London Ltd; 2&3 Profimedia.CZ s.r.o./Alamy;
7 Brian Bevan/Ardea London Ltd; 8 David Tipling/Alamy; 10 Andrew Darrington/Alamy;
13 DUNCAN USHER/FOTO NATURA/FLPA; 16 Maximilian Weinzierl/Alamy;
19 NaturePics/Alamy; 23 Getty Images/Johner Images; 24 Getty Images/Darlyne A Murawski;
29 Martin Fowler/Alamy; 31(b) Geoff Trinder/Ardea London Ltd; 35(b) Royalty-Free/Corbis;
37 Kim Taylor/Warren Photographic; 38 Tom Brakefield/CORBIS; 40 Natural Visions/Alamy;
42 Andrew Darrington/Alamy; 45 Dynamic Graphics; 48 Andrew Linscott/Alamy;
51 David Tipling/Alamy; 52 CHRIS MARTIN BAHR/SCIENCE PHOTO LIBRARY; 55 Dynamic Graphics;
56 DR JEREMY BURGESS/SCIENCE PHOTO LIBRARY; 59(b) Ian West/Oxford Scientific/photolibrary;
60 blickwinkel/Alamy; 63 CJ Wildbird Food Ltd.

ADDITIONAL ILLUSTRATORS David Ashby, Graham Austin, Bob Bampton, David Baxter,
Andrew Beckett, Joyce Bee, Isabelle Bowring, Wendy Bramall, Paul Brooks, Mark Burgess, Hilary Burn,
Liz Butler, Frankie Coventry, Patrick Cox, Kevin Dean, Sarah De Ath, Michelle Emblem, Denise Finney,
Sarah Fox-Davies, Nigel Frey, Sheila Galbraith, Will Giles, Victoria Gooman, Victoria Gordon,
David Hurrell, Ian Jackson, Roger Kent, Colin King, Deborah King, Mick Loates, Andy Martin,
Uwe Mayer, Rob McCaig, Dee McLean, Dee Morgan, David Nash, Gillian Platt, Cynthia Pow,
David Quinn, Charles Raymond, Maggie Silver, Gwen Simpson, Ralph Stobart, George Thompson,
Joan Thompson, Joyce Tuhill, Sally Volke, Phil Weare, James Woods